Finding Comfort Within the Chaos

First edition, published 2025

By Emery Rival
Copyright © 2025, Emery Rival

Paperback ISBN-13: 978-1-952685-95-8

All rights reserved. No part of this book may be reproduced or transmitted in any form or by any means, electronic or mechanical, including photocopying, recording or by any information storage and retrieval system, without written permission from the author, except for the inclusion of brief quotations in a review.

Published by Kitsap Publishing
Poulsbo, WA 98370
www.KitsapPublishing.com

Dedication

This book is dedicated to the ones who believed in hope—even when I couldn't see it for myself.

To the friends who became family, and the family who never left my side.

And to anyone standing in the dark, searching for a way out—may you find comfort in these pages and never doubt your power to bloom.

Acknowledgments

Mom
Thank you for teaching me how to stay strong and stand my ground. I love you.

You know what I mean? Jellybean.

Dad
As I walk beside you, know that everything in this life will be okay as long as we have each other. Love Ya.

Uncle
Listen up, old man: I love you, and this life wouldn't be the same without you.

Kooter
I love you; you'll never know how much. More than all the stars in all the galaxies.

Lillie
To my Mini Me: I will always be beside you in this life. No matter the situation, I got you. I love you.

Grandma Susie
I get my stubbornness from you, but I wouldn't have it any other way. Thank you for making me stand up on my own two feet and being nothing but a loving, caring mentor the whole way through. I love you.

Aunt Karen
I think about you often and thank you for your guidance.

Rebecca

I was so lost before you started to guide me. You taught me how to look at life in a healthier manner and challenged me to do things that I never thought possible. Thank you for being my serenity.

Mossy

Because of you and your loving family, I got taught structure and morals. Thank you for being such a big inspiration when I had nothing.

Tiny

To my little Salmon Biscuits: You are the biggest and best thing that has ever happened to me, but in the tiniest form. Your heart to my heart.

To the rest of my friends and family members: I wouldn't be who I am today without your love and support. I think about the ways you have changed my life every day.

Finally, I want to extend my appreciation to Kitsap Publishing for helping me shape these poems into a tangible testament of resilience and hope. This book exists because of your guidance, patience, and belief in my vision.

Above all, to anyone reading these words who feels trapped or alone—this is for you. The journey out of the dark may be long, but none of us has to walk it alone. Thank you for letting me be your friend through these pages.

Traumas eat at your mind. Whether it has to do with the loss of a loved one, heartache, feeling overwhelmed or stressed, or even fighting your head on a daily basis. I want to reach the ones who feel misled or feel like they cannot pull themselves out of an addiction because they are covering the hurt they don't want to feel, the memories they want to forget or to numb. Show them there are ways to pull through it and be strong in sobriety. That their life is not over. That they still have a chance as long as they still take air into their lungs. There is always still a chance for them to turn their lives around; some just need encouragement or to feel like they belong somewhere, anywhere but going off the rails and returning to where they have been time and time again. I want my poetry to be something that can change a life, a heart, a struggling soul.

Just like mine was.

Editorial Reviews

Finding Comfort within the Chaos by Emery Rival is about raw emotional depth, trauma, addiction, survival, and healing themes. It follows in the footsteps of the confessional poetry movement, which was started by Sylvia Plath in the mid-century. We have listed several other famous authors and poets with similar writing styles and subject matter. These authors share the emotionally raw and deeply personal approach found in this book in your hands. Their works explore similar themes of survival, addiction, mental health, and self-healing, making them excellent recommendations for readers who connect with Emery's poetry.

Courtney Peppernell — Courtney Peppernell is an Australian poet known for her heartfelt and emotional poetry collections, including the bestselling Pillow Thoughts series. Her work explores themes of love, heartbreak, healing, and self-discovery in a simple yet deeply moving style. Popular among modern poetry readers, her books offer comfort and inspiration through raw and relatable verses.

Yung Pueblo — Yung Pueblo, the pen name of Diego Perez, is a writer and poet known for his introspective and minimalist poetry on self-awareness, healing, and personal growth. His books, including Inward, Clarity & Connection, and Lighter, blend wisdom with emotional depth, encouraging mindfulness and inner peace. His work resonates with readers seeking self-discovery and transformation.

Atticus — Atticus is an anonymous poet known for his short, evocative verses on love, heartbreak, adventure, and self-discovery. His bestselling poetry collections, including Love Her Wild, The Dark Between Stars, and The Truth About Magic, blend romance and nostalgia with a modern, Instagram-friendly style. His work resonates with readers for its simplicity, depth, and emotional impact.

Sylvia Plath — Though often darker, Plath's deeply personal and evocative poetry (*Ariel*) resonates with themes of mental illness, identity struggles, and raw emotional expression.

Ocean Vuong — His poetry (*Night Sky with Exit Wounds*) and prose (*On Earth We're Briefly Gorgeous*) beautifully capture trauma, love, addiction, and survival with stunning imagery and emotional weight.

Rupi Kaur — Known for her minimalist yet deeply emotional poetry, Kaur's works (*Milk and Honey, The Sun and Her Flowers*) explore trauma, healing, and self-love in a highly accessible and impactful way.

Mary Oliver — While Oliver's poetry leans toward nature and introspection, her themes of survival, transformation, and personal growth mirror the resilience found in *Finding Comfort within the Chaos*.

Nayyirah Waheed — Like Kaur, Waheed writes in a sparse, direct style, tackling themes of identity, healing, and emotional recovery.

Jeanann Verlee — Her poetry deals with abuse, addiction, and mental illness in an unfiltered, powerful way, much like Rival's.

Introduction

Hello, my name is Emery Rival. I'm a poet, adventurer, and survivor based in the Seattle area.

When someone tells you just their name, it doesn't make much of a statement.

But if someone tells you their story—their vulnerabilities, what kicks into gear that motivation for wanting more and being more, that they came from less, from addict parents and the streets of Seattle, getting through traumas, and can still say that they are their parents' biggest advocate for getting clean and sober.

When they have their own place, and drive their own cars, and make it out into the world successfully despite what they came from, and what tried to drag them down, including phases of their own discouragement.

I am that someone. If you want to know the reasons I write, my poetry was the only thing that got me through. It got me this far by healing others and healing the worst parts of myself.

My poetry got me through sleepless nights, days where my heart was shattered, and months where my emotions were held captive by my depression and sorrow. My poetry was there for me when I would try to have conversations about how I was feeling with my parents, but they would be nodding off or disappearing for months at a time. It has been my hope, my outlet, my safe place.

What got me "here," writing to you, was not giving into my suffering when my mind had days where it had gone through enough and reached its limit. I write because there are people that have gone through similar things that they cannot talk about. I am writing as a voice to let them know "I am with you." To give them strength to stand when feeling like they are a burden to the world and need to disappear. To show them that if they feel unloved, my poetry can give them hope to find self—love and self—resilience. Because at times in my life, me being sober and an only child with addicted parents, I was lonely. I was terrified.

I want to reach people with my poetry, and speak in a raw, and unfiltered way. To be someone for people that have had suicide attempts, that have been or felt abandoned by the ones they love, and to reach out to the ones that feel like they have nothing left. I want to be the voice that can show them they are just as important as everyone else, even if they were dealt a bad hand in life.

Even as a young child, I found myself surrounded by substance abuse, domestic violence, and instability. By the time I was thirteen, I had been unknowingly introduced to opioids and spiraled into my own battle with addiction. Eventually, I ran from that life—literally jumping out of a car in an act of desperation—and began the slow, painful process of rebuilding myself from the ground up.

In my mid-teens, I faced homelessness, an unrelenting struggle with alcohol, and losing many of the people I loved around me. Including myself. For years, I blamed and punished myself, turning that pain inward through self-harm and later developing a severe eating disorder. However, despite every setback, I never lost the glimmer of hope that pushed me forward. Through therapy, the support of my friends and their families, and a fierce determination to become the person I knew I could be, I found the strength to get sober, to remain substance—free for over sixteen years, and to ultimately seek help for my eating disorder.

Today, I'm proud to say I'm healthier—physically, mentally, and emotionally—than I've ever been. I went from being homeless to sharing a home with my uncle and father, who is in recovery himself, guiding them. I'm committed to being an advocate for others who feel lost in the shadows of addiction and trauma. My poetry weaves together my darkest moments and the hope I've nurtured along the way. By speaking honestly about my experiences, I aim to remind others that no matter how deep the darkness gets, we all carry the potential to bloom.

Everything in existence, good and bad, has beautiful parts to it. The word "inspired" has a lot of meaning in itself. I have an ambition to show you that meaning.

Emory Rival

Chapters

The titles of the following chapters contain the names of flowers that bloom in the dark. They are an alluring reminder that you, too, can bloom in darkness and find comfort within the chaos.

Chapter 1: Queen of the Night: Dawn

Chapter 2: Gardenia: Detached

Chapter 3: Mock Orange: Wakefulness

Chapter 4: Casa Blanca Lily: Modify

Chapter 5: Amethyst Falls Wisteria: Revolutionize

Chapter 1

Queen of the Night

(Dawn)

Finding comfort within the Chaos

As heavy as everything is, as hard as it is to take a breath, you are worth every journey, every smile, every moment.

As heavy as everything is, you are worth the midnight drives, the 2 am cuddles, and the laughter as you get drenched in the rain.

You are worth it when you sit in silence wondering if you are enough.

There are times when it gets lighter and easier to breathe.

But in the moments where it is hard to be alive, as heavy as everything is, there is beauty in just taking in the moments as they come, as heavy as everything is sometimes you must find comfort within the chaos.

Car Wreck

Chemical abuse is like getting into a car and driving on that drug, you never know if that's going to be the last time you drive, how bad of a crash you can get into, if you will even survive and if you do survive who are you hurting around you.

It affects everyone involved when you make that initial choice.

Opinions

If someone is saying negative things about you that are not true, remember those words are just an opinion.

And that opinion only holds as much power in your head as you let it.

Peaks

Mental illness battles can feel pretty extreme from time to time.

The hardest parts that I battle throw me into episodes that make it hard to remember the reasons why I stay, my reasons at the time of these phases of madness become hidden until I snap out of it, and they come out of hiding again.

When my mental illness drags me to a different state of mind, I forget the days that are so filled with radiance they settle tucked away in spaces of my heart and soul.

Days when you breathe in the misty air after it rains.

Or memories of you throwing a snack in your backpack and you take a trip into the summer heat just to find a swimming hole.

When you have really awful days, on those days remember people that climb mountains aren't always sitting on top of its peak.

In order to climb new mountains and get to the top you have to go up and down often to get where you want to go.

If you have mental illnesses, they only grow if you feed them negativity.

—*Life hacks*

When you feel like you have missed parts of your childhood, do those things as an adult.

You are allowed to do fun things.

That smile on your face is important.

Unforgiving Streets

Some points in my life were harder than others.

And all I can do is tell you the main parts of my story that might help you in yours.

Parts that might kick in that drive in you to succeed and strive in sobriety.

The streets are unforgiving and depending on where you live, wet, snowy, and cold.

At times you could get jumped, robbed, or even be in more danger.

I only had a backpack with me.

One sweater, two pairs of pants including the ones I had on.

Only one pair of shoes.

And I considered myself lucky because some with that lifestyle don't even have shoes.

Being homeless, drug use is all around you.

Some instances if someone is trying to shout at you from the other side of the street, they are speaking their own gibberish.

Sleeping under a bridge is not an ideal home for the rest of one's life, you never know who your roommate will be day by day.

Getting food sometimes can be a challenge if you don't know what you are doing.

If you have a dog, feed your dog first.

Never fall asleep on the transit, most of the time you will end up way past your stop and have to get off in the middle of nowhere and have to find your way back.

On the streets not everyone is who they say they are, not everyone is out to help you.

Keep your belongings close to you at all times.

There are times that you walk all night because it's too uncomfortable to sleep.

The streets can turn someone desperate, and they drop some of the morals they have if they stay on them too long.

You run into situations you don't want to be a part of.

These are the things that made me want to strive to get out of that lifestyle.

You are worthy of being, safe, calm, warm, comfortable.

Healthy in all the ways you deserve.

You are not always going to like yourself, or your actions.

Resolving old baggage is hard but holding on to it for years is even harder.

Keep in mind the kind of love you show to yourself and loved ones will affect you and them until your last breath on this planet. Maybe even decades after.

Love is more powerful with memories behind it.

Those memories influence if that love is good or bad for you.

Observe people's actions, they will show you what they are choosing to be.

Before I show anger, I have to recognize first that I will have to deal with the aftermath later on.

Suffocating the flickering fire.

Stopping myself from destruction.

—Things that can be avoided

Not everything will show you beauty in this world, some things will spit venom, when life does that hold your heart close and remember the influence it can have on you and others.

—What illumes in you

Truths

Observation can be so heartbreaking when it comes to watching a loved one being dragged under by alcohol abuse.

Some call it liquid courage.

In reality it's numbing and running.

Crying to the point where your eyes burn doesn't always feel good at the time but later on you find that your soul needed that outlet.

—Holding the hurt in for too long

Motivation comes from getting sick of being stuck in the same struggles every day.

Eventually you are going to want a better life for yourself.

It is just a matter of finding your way there.

Endurance is strength.

Silence is sometimes the most brutal way to heal.

Being stuck in your head, with every negative emotion that you feel.

It's hard to love someone that is constantly not working on self—love.

They destroy themselves, while destroying you.

To know what breaks a heart

Is to know what once made it beat.

BREATHE

Breathe out your sorrows, I am here.

Breathe out your fears, I am here.

Breathe out your loss, I am forever near.

Let out all your tears, I am here.

For every emotion,

You have all of my devotion.

Breathe out the absent,

Your world is no longer silent.

If I could make you see a fragment of what I see in you,

Then you would have an extraordinary view.

I believe in you.

Breathe out, I am here.

AMBITIONS

Addiction holds a place in everyone.
   At least one time in your life,
It can be a shopping addiction,
Gambling, Your favorite hobby.
It's in the brothers of people we love
Who can't put down a needle.
It's taking over the sister you see obsessed with her boyfriend.
It's walking the streets as the person who lost
Their hopes and ambitions.
Dancing chaotically to the beat of fentanyl and meth.
Addiction is the source of broken relationships
And stolen lives that they have never lived.
At the time of heightened dependency and everyday habits,

Carelessness shows its face relentlessly.
The will to live is buried in the rubble
That they have thrown away, day after day.
Digging through the debris,
You have to find what you lost.
Your soul is in that pile of rubbish.
Take it back. Take control.
As you look back, light the match
And walk away from the dumpster fire
That once consumed you.

I have gazed at the screen of my phone way too many times

Waiting for your name to pop up on the screen

When it has stayed pitch black.

*—**The void of you***

Some don't see value in a human
   Including themselves

Ground was Ice

There is a kind of heartbreak where you don't get revived

It runs deeper than that

But you would have to rewind yourself back to the start

When you fell harder than you ever thought imaginable.

Rewind back to when the summer days were long

And we would bring our dogs to the beach

Hours where our love would never end,

But the day would

And we still had each other to hold.

We would share meals together

Ride bikes, go to museums, and get ourselves lost in the woods.

We would get Italian sodas in the morning,

And find our way into the mountains

We would sit by the river as the mist puts its cloak over

Searching for waterfalls but finding my best view was you.

Before we met, I was searching for my freedom.

But as you found me wandering, I realized I was lost. You took me and promised me safety

Promised me a home and that you would never let me go astray.

But as you led me into the dark forest and told me not to follow you back,

I realized the trees were bare and the ground under my feet was ice.

I didn't know the way back out of these dense woods.

I had gone missing because I had no idea how to find my way back to you again with no trail left behind.

I am more lost than when you found me in the first place

Because this time my heart left with you.

You walked with it.

How can I follow my heart when it has disappeared?

A phantom.

Vanished.

I lie here wanting to be revived

While my soul slowly dies.

I normally don't have my ringer turned on for my phone, but when we break up, I do.

(The love I still have for you doesn't want me to miss your call.)

I may not understand you at times, also at times my empathy is tested, but my heart still overpowers my anger from the choices you decide to make.

Is it war with you or war with myself?

—Questions I lay awake wondering

While I watch your struggles, while I watch your addictions, I see you fade, as my heart struggles to hold on, I don't want to let go of you and all the memories we have made.

Reliving Heartache

Needing to find myself again but finding the "want" or the "need" to do so seems miles away.

Looking to that point seems blurry and dripping with confusion. Confidence is severely lacking.

How do you expect myself to hold on when I feel like I have nothing to hold on for, no purpose that wants to motivate me enough, to drive worth the push, just coasting along on auto pilot, rewashing the same old memories until they are exhausted in your head.

Are feeling numb to the new memories that you have already lived before. The same places just with different people. There is a point where it turns your mind, your thoughts, and your heart dull.

Reliving heartache. At least it gives me a reason to feel something even if it is only pain, even if it is only missing a person, and even if it's only sadness, confusion, or the feeling of missing parts of you that you built with somebody else.

They walked away with those pieces that you are missing.

And you cannot tell the difference in the beginning between wanting them back or wanting those pieces back but that is the thing you must figure out when you are reliving the heartache.

Shattered Glass

I feel like shattered glass.
All these problems built up and all this time passed.
I feel like shattered glass.
Shards fell of all the pieces I used to be.
Scattered and broken, stepped on and forgotten.
I feel like shattered glass.
Once whole but broken, with a big crash.
My heart held, then smashed.
I feel like shattered glass.
All this hurt, all this pain held in.
I feel like shattered glass.
All your words imprinted on my skin; you don't know how lonely I have been.
Some days, all my mind does is spin.
It's a fight for every demon not to win.
Struggling to keep my mind stable, I wear myself thin.
Tell you where it starts?
I don't even know how to begin.
I feel like shattered glass.
Life pulling me left and to the right, with no serenity in sight.

All you want is the dark to go away and your life to be bright.

All you want is that blinding pure light.

I can't go back, and everything seems so lost.

How can I overcome all of this when I feel so tossed.

I ran away from my problems.

I ran away from my mind.

I couldn't run far enough to get away from myself.

I couldn't run far enough to hide from my heart.

From my mind.

So in my head, this is what I find.

I feel like shattered glass.

Halo

Having the ability to survive sometimes is not always my priority when I am depressed.

There are times where I just let the depths of emptiness consume my mind and let my structure crumble with it.

To sit and wonder if I am good or bad, I toss my halo, and sever off my horns because not one part of me cares at that point.

All of us have it in ourselves to be either or.

It just depends on what choices we want to make, and what part of us we choose to ignore.

Verdict in my core,

(Halo.)

Lifeless

When everything is more than you know how to bare,

When sadness and watching someone slowly kill themselves does not even give meaning to the words you want say or compare.

Lifeless.

With every hit you take, you are one moment closer to being lifeless. You let your hurt consume you enough to kill you.

Lifeless.

Breathe in the drugs.

You are one step closer to lifelessness as it hits your lungs.

I don't recognize who you are anymore.

It doesn't matter how many feelings I have in me to pour.

Recognize that you are becoming lifeless.

You're taking the beauty and everything that you are away.

You are becoming that drug, and less of my father in every way.

It affects more than just you.

Watching you do this to yourself.

It drains me. It makes me lifeless too.

Sickness in Wonderland

If you drink the vial it's all over, the one that says: DRINK ME.

It's a headache to talk to you.

It's exhausting wanting you to be better for yourself.

Every time I speak, you stitch my mouth shut.

I want to believe your lies, but I can feel the shakiness in my gut.

My voice burning to be heard by your ears.

My tears, mixed with every emotion as they continue to fall down my face.

Some hearts are not open to love.

Some were torched and when you make the journey to their heart you desire to hold,

They leave you sitting in their ashes.

They tricked you into taking the blindfold.

Loving the wrong person is lethal.

Loving the wrong person for your heart is Unorganized, Murky, Flawed, Tedious, Filled with Dancing on your Fears and Twisting your emotions and beliefs.

But overall, above everything, making it so you Question who you are as a person and what Is reality even doing to you.

Getting through the haze in your mind of what is factual and has truth or staying in their wonderland.

Because everything up until this point they built for you to believe.

I don't want to be in wonderland anymore, everything is built the same here and full of lies.

One maker, one ruler, wonderland is for the weak and crazy.

Surrounded by the caterpillars sitting on the mushrooms doing drugs to understand life more and trying to make these issues magically disappear.

If you drink the vile it's all over, the one that says: DRINK ME.

Get me out of wonderland and away from you, This place sucks.

Your world is warped.

Just like you. And just like you want me to be.

Screw you, I will be out free.

Other people can jump into that rabbit hole.

But not me.

Never again.

Never again.

Never again.

Fierce

On my worse of days, life has a funny way of saying to me, look at the destruction I have made, be devastated. Clean it up.

And I want to just look at life and give it my middle finger.

It is valid to feel like this on these days.

Silver linings don't always come, so occasionally you will have to make your own.

And often People will do things to make you angry, because let us face it, as humans we all have our selfish moments, at least one time or another.

Some of us like to even play that selfish card repetitively.

And that can get old fast.

Fairness is not always present.

If I were to sit across from life in these moments, trust me I would make it known it deserves the death glare and an eye roll.

But part of dealing with these days is remembering that we are capable of being adults, and handling situations with patience, because we deserve to show ourselves gentleness in these moments when all seems too much to manage.

Be gentle to yourself and know on these days you are fierce.

Depression

When the Depression hits, I can't be the only one.

I can't be the only one that feels like reaching all their goals are for nothing because sooner or later you die anyway so what was the point in going so far?

When the depression hits, I can't be the only one. That reaches for different scenarios in their mind on how it could have all been changed before getting to this point.

When the depression hits, I can't be the only one. As it feels like someone has taken over your body making you paralyzed. A sort of toxin runs through your veins making you immobile. You just don't want to get up.

When the depression hits, I can't be the only one. That their favorite place in the entire world's their room isolating away from anything that could ever hurt you again.

When the depression hits, I can't be the only one. That feels everything at once and then nothing at all. An overwhelming sadness like you wish you could tell everybody sorry for even existing.

When the depression hits, I can't be the only one. To reach down and find the strength to back off, because moods are forever shifting.

In Between

I sat here thinking the best way I can Illustrate mental illness if I had too,

When I get depressed, I see shades, when my mental illness lays dormant, I feel like I see every color there ever was.

It feels like you are being tortured when everything in you does not want to love or care for a person, but you still do.

Moons

The moon is bright, but still sits in darkness.
That doesn't mean it lost its vibrance or its value.
It is there to make everything else illuminate too.

___

Remember Me

Remember me when I was strong.

Remember me instead of All the things that made me flawed.

Remember me when a sunset hits.

Remember me and not the mentally ill fits.

Remember the smile that you adore.

Not me as all my tears hit the floor.

Remember my heart and how it loves you.

Not the rage that consumes me, and my anger too.

Remember me as I find my way, this is me taking it day by day.

That's all I have right now to hold on.

So, remember me when I was strong.

Rupture

As my mind blares, there is an outer layer of me that is on edge and ever rougher.

Cracking on the inside and begging to rupture.

Pleading to be un-imprisoned.

I think about the paths that lead me to my fate.

And looking back on every road that I decided to take.

I am here.

And my mind blares.

I swear having mental illnesses always comes in pairs.

You can't have one illness without an attachment to it.

Not just anxiety.

Not just depression.

Not just PTSD.

Not just an eating disorder.

Wait.

Wait for the split.

The split can come with identity disorders.

Trauma. Breakdowns.

As my mind blares, there is an outer layer of me, constantly trying to protect myself.

Begging not to rupture.

Shards of Me

If I close my eyes and drown out the world.

If I sit in silence and focus on the functioning beats of my heart, it whispers these things to me.

You have not protected me.

You have lent me out only to receive parts of me back worn, torn, shredded, thrashed and humiliated.

You have put me in relationships that made me feel intimidated.

You have made me go back even when I felt annihilated.

All the beautiful words you tell me, you lack to show actions within your partners.

I need you to grow and be a lot smarter.

There are only shards of me left, save them before I stop beating in your chest.

I am tired of sitting in your mess.

I am fed up with the hurt and depressed.

The rhythm is too loud for you not to hear me.

I pump life into your soul.

Trust me and build back everything in me they stole.

I love you, and I need you to pull through.

I need you to love yourself, and give me the chance to flourish too.

Sometimes I can't tell if everyone else around me that is unstable.

Or if it's just me that is.

Maybe both.

> **—The things we need to work on with grace**

The worse memories of you painted in my mind,

But loving you is all my heart seems to find.

> **—*Conflicted***

Ghost

I can feel it in my core.

I sit alone at night.

My dreamcatcher has no defense against what floods my mind, when I try to lay my head down on my pillow and unwind.

As sleep calls me into the deep.

I know it's about to get really unsafe, while I walk the halls into the mouth of madness.

Begging for my dreams not to show me visions of my sadness.

My Night terrors always start the same way.

I am standing still.

I am breathing heavily.

I can hear my heart's velocity in my chest.

My lungs feel like frost as it is, I can see the condensation hitting the freezing air as I breathe.

The sky, the moon gazing at me, with a grey night scene.

In this frame that my dream sets It must be winter, because everything including the heart you show is ice.

You stand in front of me, as I beg for you not to throw my soul into devastation.

Speaking with such hollow words.

Telling me it is her you want, and that I don't hold

your heart anymore.

That you are walking away and leaving my mind in a cold war.

In the End my fate always Runs the same.

I put on me the blame.

Then they start to creep in.

Voices.

Leading me to my grave.

I call for you, but I am never saved.

You walk away, you went ghost.

Vanishing when I needed you the most.

The only voice after, that is silent in my dream is yours.

I look down at my hands as they shake.

But the whispers turn to screaming as they lead me to my fate.

A scenery of moments flash through me as I sleep.

I don't notice, in reality I cry out and weep.

No matter where I go everyone is always decaying after you leave.

Here comes my last scene.

In my dream.

Different ways to die, like an overdose on morphine.

Velvet Petals

In the beginning you were breathtaking.

Your personality is soft and weightless like velvet petals.

Your comforting touch and conversations drew me in.

You always had time to make me laugh, to hold me close, to let me share the things with you that meant the most.

As we started to shift and change, we started battling each other and felt drained.

Sleepless nights and voided days, as we split one thing remains, soft weightless like velvet petals of a rose, in the chamber of my heart my love for you always glows.

Go seek the world out, go live your life, go find another to love and grow with, because like a rose you are still breathtaking.

To everyone that has ever experienced this kind of loss, I hope you heal from your heart aching, and overcome the negative thoughts.

Love Ya

When you choose your dose.
    I still cared.
When it became a way of escape within you.
I fought for you to stay and not chase the high.
When it became your obsession.
I became insignificant.
When it devoured the person I knew.
It fueled my darkest fears.
You let this go on for all these years.
I sacrificed my happiness to help you always.
When your addiction wouldn't just wash away.
It flooded my entire existence.
Begging you to reflect.
But it is forcing me to adapt.
To be carried on as a choice.

It has always been a choice.

Change is always better than the alternative.

Dying, I don't get you back.

There's no reversing those effects.

So, tell me what happens next.

I'm done with this being so complex.

When you choose your dose.

You are robbing yourself of life.

Get clean, you're so close.

I don't want to see you overdose.

If that's not enough for me to say,

to try to make you stay.

Then you need to know I will love

you until your last day.

Chapter 2

Gardenia

(Detached)

A Lesson

Living through the days I have found I spiral when I don't build structure for myself.

Setting goals is a must, even small ones.

Goals give you things to work towards, more things to look forward to.

You absolutely are worthy of those goals.

You can reach them.

All the doubt you might have had in yourself, lose all that doubt.

Because you make your own choices, and only you will be able to destroy that doubt within.

And when you do that, then you realize you can do anything with all your heart and soul.

With passion, with an unconditional burning flame inside of you.

Doubt is not a friend; it is a lesson.

GLIMPSES OF YOU

They Evoke my mind.

I haven't see you in months.

The last words I said to you were unkind.

Out of anger maybe, but how do you expect me to feel,

When nothing but sober memories of you seems real.

I know we all didn't ask to be on this earth.

But making the best of everyday while we are here is better than living in constant misery.

COMMIT

A commit alters a structure in a galaxy.
   Leading to changes like star formations.
It's a notable moment in a galaxy evolution.
You are like a commit.
Bursting with all of the fire inside of you.

DESERT

If you have ever seen the Atacama Desert after it rains, it is filled with blooming flowers.

Millions of seeds sitting there waiting to evolve.

The rain may bring thunder and darkness but afterwards the flowers are thriving and radiant.

—Don't give up until you bloom

Freedom

Addictions take you over, when it gets really off the wall, you wake up and the first thing you think about when you're out of your drink or substance is how you will acquire more. At times you spend all day figuring out how to get money for it, or finding it. In sobriety you don't have to worry about having that weight over you.

You don't have to worry about having that time stolen from you day after day, just to get that fix.

No matter if you get sober on your own, or ask for help.

Inpatient.

Outpatient.

Groups.

Therapy.

Or any source of help to be clean and stay clean.

You did it and have your freedom.

But most importantly you have the tools now to be a version of yourself you lost in the dependency.

And that my friend is something to celebrate every day.

REALITY

I think society has this misconception of happiness.

Like we are supposed to be nothing but happy constantly.

But in reality, that is not how life is.

Life hits us with blind sidedness on occasion.

Many instances will be out of our hands.

Unhinged at times.

Happiness always travels back to you.

And stays beside you when it can.

Like a best friend.

Walk to Me

Change happens when you know you can't stand one more day of the same thing, or how it has been.

It can be when you have crumbled and have lost everything that once mattered.

Could also be when the void screams so loud inside you it keeps you up till 5 am.

What do you do if you can't stand the thought of being in your own skin anymore?

That's when change stares at your hollow face.

And says let me put life back into you.

Walk to me.

———————————————

It is never going to be easy when you have been through trauma, and you battle forces that try and draw you down. Search for your inner beauty, your trauma doesn't define you, you make the choices everyday to define yourself.

What I have learned over my lifetime is that having parents addicted to substances over anything else, let them know you love them, but you don't love their choices.

My biggest fear was losing them unexpectedly and not letting them know that.

Specifying you still love them always, but you don't agree with the lifestyle.

And want more for them.

When I tell you that you are absolutely capable of anything to better yourself, I mean every word.

If you told me to choose something like a color for myself, I wouldn't choose a color, I would choose to be iridescent, because I always know I have the capability of change.

—Like a phenomenon

___

You don't always have to understand someone's choices or agree with them.

But you can work on fighting the ways you let it affect you.

_____

Wildflower

I lay here with the lights down, feeling paralyzed.

Looking back, my flower blooming with pedals of emotions.

So filled with designs of color.

Each pedal shows a memory of how you used to love me.

Scented with comfort and raindrops of safety

And happiness filled my vase.

As time took its course, you sat my flower up in the window.

I rarely got sunlight before you decided to clip at my leaves.

You once telling me I was one-of-a-kind

And how beautiful I was.

Now you are sitting here claiming

I am a wilted.

With my pedals disintegrating into ash

You talk down to me.

Because I'm not the same flower you picked in the beginning.

Crispy brownish—black tips

No nourishment running through my veins

You snapped my stem when I grew thorns.

Everything inside of me mourns

For that flower I used to be.

But instead, you take what's left of my stem

And place it on my grave.

There is nothing about me that you alone could save.

As my friends are grieving, they pick up my stem and plant me in the ground

All over again.

As time passes and you have other bouquets,

I will simply be in the ground

Regrowing my ways.

For now, I am a wildflower

So wrap your tight ribbons around your bouquets

And sprinkle your holy water on them to keep them alive.

I am rooted in the ground
   And will not die.
You will ask yourself why they did not live a long life,
It's because you tamed them.
Cut off the beauty for yourself.
For I am not ugly,
For I have grown.
Keep sitting there with your wilted bouquets
And your heart made of stone.
I'm sitting deep in the forest now
With sunshine, loved and grown.

Love Anyway

Silence makes you reflect

And it makes you walk the path to finding out who you are

Loving with your whole heart

Even though not everyone's heart is capable of the same type of love.

That's sacrifice.

And still loving yourself through all the complications that the world throws at you

Shows your endurance.

Everybody has flaws

But we live anyway.

We love anyway.

We feel anyway.

Learn how to mold those flaws into lessons

Courage and the strength to be patient with yourself

For some people, the wounds are a lot deeper than you can see.

Some bleed internally,

Not showing a thing on the outside.

Let your heart grow with patience and understanding.

If someone is not willing to meet you halfway for help when it comes to substances, often there is nothing you can do to change that.

Until they want to change themselves.

    Let them lose the stability you give them, often times they will fight for that stability back.

    Thinking at the time they had nothing to lose, and figured out later on that it was a lie they told themselves.

    —Know your value and show others that value too.

Downpour of Symphonies

As I lay down in the forest, the evergreen trees surround me.

Drenched by the rain, I feel at ease.

Glossy boulders around and a trout filled stream.

These are the kind of days that set my heart truly free.

The sounds of rainwater trickling down the sides of the rocky cliffs.

Puddles, downpour of symphonies and ripples containing moving art.

Usually, memories and trauma tear me apart.

But here nature covers me with her calming blanket.

Some days it's hard to think I will even make it.

Solitude in a serene, wooded clearing.

My heart sits in my chest as I am settled on the ground.

Beating with nature.

Alive as my surroundings.

I feel it.

A life inside everything, flourishing, just like me.

Wild.

But at peace and free.

NOT A VICTIM

In this world, feeling like I want to decay,

working on my traumas but needing to figure out what's left of me to save.

It's hard to breathe it hard to cope, and every time I try to say how I feel from start to close,

It's just noise. Overcrowding my head. Even talking about my traumas is something I dread.

But I want to break the cycle. Of the heaviness that weighs me down.

You're not taking me with you, I will not drown.

You see, am not me when I'm around you, and that's your choice doing all the drugs that you do.

I've let you chain me for far too long, I am choosing me this time, and I will stand strong.

I am not a victim anymore.

—Know what you want to define you.

Forest

The best days I hold dear in my soul are when I hear the rain hit the lake.

When I walk into the woods, I am completely isolated by myself.

The feeling when I take the palm of my hand and run it across the wet leaves.

Days where my shoes get ruined, my hair gets Drenched and all I have is myself as I look up at the rain falling down through the trees.

The best days I hold dear in my soul, is with the Forest and me.

Growth

When you open your heart up to things, that takes a lot of courage.

People get hurt, people run and numb their issues.

Fractured people tend to Fracture other people.

They don't always mean to fracture others, but they will do so until they take on the challenge to face their issues within themselves.

Growth is uncomfortable.

But if you are not growing, then you are sitting stagnant.

Never moving, never learning, never changing.

Relationships will fail time and time again.

Because growth opens the heart to what we block out, what we hide from, our fear of the unknown.

Fear of becoming different than what we have always known.

When you open your heart up to yourself, believe in your fullest potential.

You work on your fears and you start to flourish.

Then everything around you does too.

You start to carry yourself differently.

When you open your heart up, it makes room for change.

Compassion, belief, faith in yourself, trust in who you can become to your fullest extent.

Once you find the inner qualities, they kick into gear the drive to know better, to love better, to do better.

—That's growth.

Rivers

A river must run its course to meet the ocean.

It does not sit stagnant like a lake.

It flows as the rocks filter out the parasites and toxins.

Its journey is unexpected and great.

Passing through all the obstacles, down mountain sides, plummeting off high cliffs.

Falling, and falling hard into the unknown.

Taking risks and drifting to its fate.

Sometimes calm, sometimes crashing awake.

We flow through life like rivers, not knowing our destinations.

Always flowing toward something more that we want to become, moving past the rapids we are escaping from.

Views

There are times in your life when you will second guess your choices and decision making.

Then there are times where you will second guess them again.

Sometimes the path does not always have a clear view.

Some days you become more fragile than you would like to admit, but I encourage you to carry through.

Those times where you do not mean to just lose it.

Climbing to get to the summit.

Do not quit and cause yourself to Plummet.

On the days that can trigger those thoughts that put doubt in your head, I am going to be real with you, unfiltered and advice that should not be left unsaid.

Life will not always favor you.

It will not always show you mercy.

But it will show you lessons and build your character.

This helps as you walk through life.

Your choices are limitless.

No pressure to move mountains.

Just travel through the beauty and elements.

Tred, climb, and advance to your peak ability.

To hike up to Tranquility.

Life at its extremes will challenge every aspect of your being.

Get to your destination, you have the adaptivity to ascend to the sights and views worth your while.

At the finish you will come to find it was worth every mile.

Vast Oceans

When it came to Addiction, I never believed at the time that I could be more.

I relapsed repetitively.

Until one day the realization came over me.

My mind had to overpower the pain, the loss, the sadness.

Restricted.

Conflicted.

Drowning my entirety.

Like a cargo ship carrying all this weight.

Sinking this ship is what it would take.

I didn't want to be this me anymore.

I was ready to start this war.

I wanted to be more like a sailboat.

Free.

Away from the shores.

With the waves carrying my fate.

I knew my sobriety was something to celebrate.

New vast oceans.

Came all new emotions.

Free, no longer kept in that black sea.

I made the choice to discover me, and sail away from my old identity.

As I navigate towards serenity.

You are the breathing Art.

The one that walks with emotion, charm and charisma, whether you put your mind and soul, heart and breath into sheet music, an instrument, soundtracks, song writing, poetry, painting, pottery, or your favorite hobby.

The strength behind it is you.

Chapter 3
Mock Orange

(Wakefulness)

Breaking Shackles

Codependency is hard when it goes hand and hand with an addiction.

Think about it, not depending on a person, but on the drink or substance.

That drink and or substance asks so much from you.

All the things you give up.

Let's breathe through this list as we read carefully.

Your genuine self.

Breathe.

Family.

Breathe.

Your health.

Breathe.

Now let's pinpoint the reality.

A drink or substance that you may indulge in to feel an illusion of happiness.

Reread the word again.

Illusion.

Drugs take you to a different place, that isn't reality.

Held captive in the shackles.

When breaking the heavy chains.

Deep down your conscience, your heart, personality, and individuality wants to be unconfined.

Unsupervised.

Blossoming into a creative love and safe place for yourself.

SHALLOW BREATHING

I t was sunny out today.

The sky was beautiful.

The people were wearing summer clothes.

Walking their dogs.

Driving with the windows down with the music blaring and their sun glasses on.

But in these moments, all I could think about was you.

In the hospital, fighting for your life.

Shallow breathing and a heavy heart.

I miss you.

The way you were.

The way you would say my name.

The way you would want to go on a hike.

The way you got excited whenever I would cook you dinner because you were hungry.

I miss watching our favorite cartoons.

And most of all I miss your presence.

What do you do when the person that tells you it's all going to be okay, isn't okay?

You are there for them and tell them to stay strong and you too will be there when everything goes wrong.

Changed Fate

Closing your eyes and thinking if you ever lost a person and they passed on, reliving that pain, if you use and something happens to you, you are putting that same feeling on to someone else that was close to you.

If you don't want to let go of the someone that passed on, someone doesn't want to let go of you.

If you go through days of missing them, remember someone would miss you too.

Only you hold the power to change that fate.

Nobody wants to lose a loved one to an Overdose.

PHASES

Chaos can be over-stimulating for your functioning mind.

Anxiety happens.

When you find your mind glitching due to PTSD or a trigger, these things might help calm you.

Putting a cold rag on your forehead, the cold compress helps your mind focus on something else like the temperature.

Taking a hot bath will calm your nerves.

Reading.

Taking a walk.

Writing down anything that comes to your mind just to vent it out.

A cozy blanket.

Also, a hot cup of tea with honey.

Don't be harsh on yourself in these moments.

Everyone feels overwhelmed sometimes.

Feelings do pass and always change like the weather.

Phases.

It won't last forever.

Cinders

Something about sitting next to a campfire the scent of cedar burning, the heat holding your face, and crackling sounds as the cinder burns vivid.

Even fires can go wild and can't be tamed.

When your soul wants to fight to pick yourself up let it.

Let it go wild and untamed.

Make it burn everything in your path that was once holding you back from anything but being remarkable.

WHISPERS OF REBECCA

If loving, you enough was all I needed to do to "save you."

You would have been saved from your addiction a long time ago.

It's not that I'm not enough, it's your lack of expectations within yourself.

With You

When someone abandons you due to an addiction, it is easy to blame yourself.

Please remember they are going through their own battles.

They have not found self—love or care yet.

That does not have anything to do with you.

Yes, it hurts, because we all long for a healthy relationship and have greater expectations for that person than they even realize to have for themselves.

And that's the hard reality of it.

You are not alone with that.

Many experience that with their loved ones too.

Lost on Purpose

Leave on a journey one day with the intention of getting lost.

Take that drive.

Take that unknown road that guides you to a destination that takes your breath away.

That ties with your soul.

That gives you relief from the stress you've been keeping in.

When a certain part of you that hates everything, you have become before you get better, collaborates with the parts of you that has resilience and finds the drive in you to change, that's when you meet perseverance.

When you don't want to push yourself and you want to admit defeat, that's the time that matters the most to get back up on your feet.

People can guide you and have a part in it but in the end.

No one is going to do it for you, except you.

When you become sober and stay sober you will find there are always upgrades in life that come with doing that for yourself.

—*Big and small achievements*

JUST AS IMPORTANT

When I feel like the world is against me and I need to leave, I tell myself this is just an emotion at this moment. It comes and goes, it passes, sometimes it lingers longer, and I battle it for days and maybe even months as it whispers to me, and it may come back and say mean things to me like a bully. But that doesn't mean that you need to give that voice power, that voice hold lies. You belong here just as much as everyone else on this planet. And don't you ever forget that.

Loving myself was the hardest place to get to, I walked every path I swear, before I found that one.

But I can tell you now this path I am on is the most beautiful one with the best scenery.

My Secret

I have been an addict at one point in my life, and I can tell you it is a choice.

You make that choice to pick up that bottle, to pick up that substance.

To keep doing it over and over.

You want to know a secret?

You are stronger than your addiction.

Alternate Ending

Are you even living

When you don't remember yesterday?

Are you even living

When you are running from the potential that you have?

Are you even living when you stop searching for the love you long for within yourself?

Unbury yourself before the drugs make your loved ones bury you.

Because when that happens, no one deserves that situation.

So many things could have been changed, and many things were left unsaid, unfinished.

This is not how anyone that has love for you wants your book to end.

Losing yourself is a tragedy, but finding yourself again and being healthy is a statement all in its own.

—Strength

Destruction comes when you run from what is hurting you and don't get the tools to cope with the trauma. Ignorance does not always come with bliss. You have the ability to free what's locked you down all these years. And that version of you is something you're never going to want to miss.

Just because you have the ability to have a child doesn't mean you are ready and know how to take care of one with stability.

Sometimes building inner strength comes hand-in-hand with agony.

Some days, I would give anything to die

And other days, I would give anything to have more time.

It is worth the stay.

—*The faces you would miss*

Clouded

I can relate a lot to clouds.

On my darkest of days, I experience the dense weight of despair, as the sense of keeping everything in is beyond overwhelming.

The mass is the size of the sky.

Clouds keep moving, they keep cycling.

They collect, evaporate, condensate, and precipitate.

Think about it.

You take on other people's problems and fix, help and want the outcome to be happiness.

Thats always the goal.

Their happiness.

Collect.

You take it all in along with your own stuff and try and find a fix.

A conclusion, a better ending.

Evaporating dilemmas.

Holding in all this vapor, all these secrets, all these complexities, that make you feel hazed over.

Condensate.

This one's, my favorite.

Let it go.

Make your soul pour.

Get it all out of you.

The thing is, you can care about other people's problems, but if they Arnt willing to motivate themselves and want to change you will be the one suffering for it.

Let that all wash away until they are willing to step up with you.

Until they can show you, they matter to themselves, and you matter to them too.

Precipitate.

Clouds have the power and force of nature.

Be that force too.

Annihilated

When your heart feels annihilated.

You lose a sense of your own self, a form of your own Identity sometimes.

You lose passion for anything that once mattered.

When you are apart from the person you once knew, apart from the memories that brought you together, apart from the back and forth, then I love you, but I hate you, then I can't live without you, apart from the fact that I never want to see you again.

When your heart feels annihilated.

This rupture happens, you hit a point where most of the time it causes destruction within yourself and you just collapse.

When your heart feels annihilated.

There's a different kind of tone to your whole being.

A part of you that senses only the one that annihilated your heart in the first place, can be the only one that can assemble the pieces back to fit.

When your heart feels annihilated, remember all the reasons why that person loved you from the start, and learn to fall in love with those reasons too.

Inspiration Comes Within

What inspires someone?

It could be when they are at their lowest point, and feeling like their only option is to see the end.

It could be the loss of someone in their life that made them feel things so beautiful, so magnificent in a different light that no one else gave them that push, showed them that drive, the beauty in the world that they once were missing, they found within a person, so it set fire within their soul.

Inspiration comes within.

It comes with many different views, many different thoughts, and a whole lot of overwhelming feelings.

It can come with losing everything at a price, and enough drive to want to gain a better you as you build.

Inspiration comes within.

The Lighthouse

You may feel at your lowest now.

My lighthouse.

Shining your light as far as it can go, over the sea.

When I am lost in my storms, guiding me through the instability.

Showing me, I need to keep going until I find my way and conquer the storm.

Glaring your light across the deep, as the tides roll in and sweep the shore.

As soon as I see a glimpse of your lighthouse, I know from then on, I'm not alone anymore.

The sea has taken so many Tragedies.

Down Under they all go.

But my little lighthouse beams, so I can always safely find my way back home.

Shred

You wake up one day and you are just here.

You did ask to be here; you were not developed enough to understand what here even means.

But one day you are going though things at a premature age just knowing what you are going through is not quite right.

And wither you like it or not as you are growing, pain becomes recognizable.

Then you get thrown into this mess of questions that like to pace through your head; what did I do to deserve this? Why am I here? What is the purpose? What is my purpose? Why wasn't I dealt a better hand in life?

The answers to all these questions.

If you do not go through, or deal with, every single aspect of things that have built you in your life, you would not be individually you.

Life makes you develop certain emotions that come to define you in your stages of growing.

That's what we all must remember through this whole journey.

Even on the heaviest of days you want to, try not to shred your being apart.

The thing about Advice is, it is up to you as a person if you want to take someone's Advice or leave it.

Advice is always suggestions.

Sometimes we forget the last decisions come down to ourselves, and what route we make the choices to take.

CHAPTER 4
Casa Blanca Lily
(Modify)
SHIFTING CHANGES

Low days are definitely going to happen, that is inevitable.

Having a series of bad things happen one after another, that happens too.

When you experience those happy moments that deafens the heartache, keep pushing through.

All that is worth living for never comes easy.

Finding out your strengths is challenging.

We have to have armor when it comes to battling our addictions, fear of what could be without our crutches holding us up.

But I promise you, you can walk without that crutch, it takes willpower.

If you made the choice to do the substance, you can also make the choice to be without it.

Walking away from many things in this life can be heavy, but the opposite word of fragile is strong.

Patience.

You are okay to feel, to break down, to leave the crutch behind you, and all the emotions that come with that.

One shifting change at a time.

SOBRIETY

One of the hardest things I had to go through when getting sober was cutting off my friend group.

Not because I didn't care about them, but I had to care about my sobriety.

Distancing sometimes is better to help you not relapse.

When you get to a point where you don't ever want to touch the substance or drink again, then you know other people's habits don't waver your choices anymore.

That's when you can make the choice if you still want them in your life or keep walking separate ways.

Some don't ever walk the path of sobriety, but what I have learned through my years, that path no matter what the outcome is it never ends well.

For them, or the loved one in their life.

Struggling with overdoses, making choices you wish you could take back, hurting people that want to help, lying, hiding, stealing, doing things the sober you wouldn't even dream of doing.

You may feel like you want to die sometimes, but I promise you when death actually looks back at you, all the reasons to stay alive start flooding in.

Speaking into Existence

My dad always says to me when I tell him I'm getting a cold don't put more thought into that because you don't want to put it into existence.

Meaning If I think I'm starting to get sick, If I actually believe I'm getting sick, I will actually be sick.

Maybe it's the same thing when your mental illness spirals, If I say I'm getting worse and speak it into existence out loud it will make it become truer.

—Things to contemplate

Maybe sometimes you want to not think about everything else in the world and the people that effect you and once in a while that's okay.

Breaks are needed. Taking time for yourself is a must.

If you are not giving yourself periods of grace, how will you ever be able to heal yourself fully.

Rewiring Yourself

Getting into a place in sobriety where you don't want to relapse is hard.

Remember to give yourself patience.

If it's your first day of sobriety or 15 years of being sober, you have accomplished so much.

Not everyday is going to feel good.

Days will come when you have a full out war with yourself and your head.

It comes with rewiring your brain.

Transforming all the harmful thoughts into loving thoughts takes time.

Day one or 15 years later, you are worth being healthy for yourself and experiencing everything incredible that this life has to offer.

And I know you have it in you.

One moment at a time.

If a person wants to change their toxic actions and traits, if they are really remorseful for hurting you, then in the end they will take those steps and make efforts to actually show themselves and you results and not harm the relationship they have with you.

I try to keep in the back of my mind when I have a disagreement with someone, I need to watch what I say back because you never know if that's going to be the last time you get to talk with them.

Your words have meaning and, in some instances, you can't take harsh words back.

—Things we have to live with

Remind yourself when you're working on inner things not to work on it all at once, so you don't feel discouraged or overwhelmed.

—Everything worth having takes patience.

Scenery

Some of the ways to heal yourself from past pain, is focusing on the things that make you the happiest.

Getting lost in the woods sometimes helps you find yourself.

Knowing no one is around you.

And you can just be you for once.

And take in the scenery.

The most frustrating moment sometimes is wanting to say something to someone, trying to voice what hurts, and getting attacked without them taking the time to hear out the reasons why, first.

Patience — *an everyday skill to work on.*

Whatever hurts you in life, it helps to put that hurtful energy towards something positive, use it to drive to push yourself harder, for better opportunities in your life.

There is always room to step up in the things you want to achieve.

Whatever task you focus on, it will have a greater outcome than when you first started.

Just like working on oneself, you just get better the more you focus on that task at hand.

When feeling shattered due to other's actions, that is the most dire time to do something for yourself.

—Self-care matters

Unfold yourself and find the beauty you have been hiding from the world.

If you hold on to love tighter than your addiction, you will figure out what one matters to you more, what one is healthier for you, and what one will guide you to a better path for yourself. If you want to let go of the hurt, and the bad, you can start by letting go of your addiction. It won't be easy, but it comes with a lot of beautiful things if you give it time.

Love yourself like you love the beauty of a flower.

As you watch it grow, you will see it bloom and open up more.

Results

I know when you walk into therapy, it's never easy, but their overall job is to help you bloom into the best version of your authentic self.

It is hard to open up to anyone when you've been lied too for so long.

It's hard to face what keeps you up at night.

What looks back at you in the mirror every day when you are not kind because all that's replaced that kindness up until now is anger.

The anger is there, but it's the hurt that you haven't defeated that's got the hold on you.

Understand that you just want happiness. And you are not a burden.

Let them help you, because you want to help yourself.

If you keep going the way you have with your anger, then you will never see new results in happiness.

Sometimes, when you feel so small,
That makes more room to grow.

___

BATTLEGROUND

The greatest battle in life is within yourself.

You will battle your mind more than anyone you will come across.

Confidence in yourself is so easy to toss.

If you haven't found love for yourself, then most days will feel endless and harsh.

Tearing every bit of you apart.

All the way down to how you look when you smile.

The art of learning to love yourself, when you constantly hate yourself, can take a while.

It's easy to drown oneself, when in your head you feel the problem is always you.

But please, you must know none of those negative thoughts are true.

There is beauty in every mood you have, because in some ways it builds your character.

If you do not live through these moods, through these thoughts, you will never find clarity.

It is a gift to feel.

It is a gift to change.

To rise.

Some people don't make it.

They quit.

But how will you find who you truly want to become if you give in?

That person lies within you.

Somewhere.

The greatest battle in life is within yourself.

Find yourself and learn to love all the messy parts that bring you there.

I know your heart hurts; I know you are tired of this battle.

I know it feels endless and exhausting.

You are still searching, and that's okay.

As long as you don't cut your time short impulsively.

You deserve mercy,

When you have been lost for so long.

Life is a journey, that's what we are all here for.

And you need to stay strong.

The greatest battle in life is within yourself.

Find, Love, grow, and be gentle.

To many souls out there, your value is so sentimental.

The Serpent

How vibrant your colors flow, as you slither through the grass.

No one knowing the obstacles you've gone through to get to this place in your life and through the past.

The hills, valleys, plains, and cliffs have heard your sorrows and dusk never promised you any tomorrows.

You make journeys day by day, shedding all the incredible parts that got you here, shedding all the wounds that impacted you.

Feeling your way through the grasslands, you have gone miles from where you first started.

Growing.

Moving every day towards new heights and views.

Like the serpent, don't let anything stop you from surviving.

Even though sometimes this planet isn't always inviting.

There is a whole world out there waiting for you to shed and grow.

While you make your path, the sun's opalescent light finds you.

Let your vibrant colors show.

The most challenging task is self-love.

—*Worth*

Searching

When you have gone through life with heaviness and heartbreak, abandonment, and neglect, when you have been lied to, and the people you've cared for the most reflect the most toxic version of themselves on to you.

It runs through you, makes you question if you should be around, makes you lose your own worth in your own eyes, because if the closest to you don't see your worth, what makes you worthy?

It's like your self—love is replaced with knowledge and strength, you learn how to see through the deception, learn how to cope on a day—to—day basis with the mentally ill, you learn what makes you stronger, what your trauma triggers are, what makes you go awol.

You learn how to pick yourself up when no one else would.

And maybe that's a form of self—love that we overlook in times where we feel like one's world is shattered.

Self—love has different views.

We just have to search to see them.

We are all Diverse

But some of the vast things that bring us together are the same things that, let me remind you, could make humanity smile.

Listening to a song on repeat because it draws something out of you that you have held within.

We are all Diverse.

Yet we all feel the same emotions during our life, just different times and different situations and experiences.

In our lifetimes, diverse or not, we all feel loss, we all feel loneliness, expression is nothing to be ashamed of.

We are all diverse. Yet we all cried.

We have all wanted and longed for something more.

We have all had sleepless nights, and broken hearts.

We are all diverse.

But we reach to find comfort in things that have meaning to us, sometimes good, sometimes not so good.

Not one of us is a whole copy of another.

I encourage you to seek every day more of who you are, the art of being you is building as a masterpiece.

You are the canvas, the paint, and the brush.

You get to be as abstract as you want to be.

You are a creation.

We are all diverse.

But we are all human.

Chapter 5
Amethyst Falls Wisteria

(Revolutionize)

A Lesson

Living through the days I have found I spiral when I don't build structure for myself.

Setting goals is a must, even small ones.

Goals give you things to work towards, more things to look forward to.

You absolutely are worthy of those goals.

You can reach them.

All the doubt you might have had in yourself, lose all that doubt.

Because you make your own choices, and only you will be able to destroy that doubt within.

And when you do that, then you realize you can do anything with all your heart and soul.

With passion, with an unconditional burning flame inside of you.

Doubt is not a friend; it is a lesson.

Supremacy

The part about getting sober that was the hardest for me was not knowing what kind of person I would be after, I let something eat up years of my life and I was used to that, used to the late nights of not feeling my pain, mornings of ignoring my thoughts and just only wanting my next high and my mind to shift away from the thoughts and feelings that I buried down 10 feet under.

Afraid of facing everything and feeling vulnerable and uncomfortable.

You know what though?

It is not impossible to do.

Supremacy over what you run.

Not what you let run you.

Restoring yourself is worth the risk of the unknown.

I know we all didn't ask to be on this Earth.

    But making the best of everyday while we are here is better than living in constant misery.

Losing yourself is a Tragedy, but finding yourself again and being healthy is a statement all in its own.

—strength

You are the Breathing Art

The one that walks with emotion, charm and charisma, whether you put your mind and soul, heart and breath into sheet music, an instrument, soundtracks, song writing, poetry, painting, pottery, or your favorite hobby.

The strength behind it is you.

Story

If I told you all of my story up until this point in my life, I would not be lying to you when I say most of me would want to erase it and rewrite the whole memoir over again.

If I told you that I was in love with my story, that would be a lie too.

If you asked me if I have learned a lot from my story, I would tell you each chapter was, and still is, a lesson that unfolds.

Some moments I have the incredible urge to burn the whole book and watch the flames consume every page.

All of my wounds would become ash.

And the aftermath of who I ever was or who I might become will be gone with the embers.

But that is not me.

I will not give in to misery.

I survive my own story.

The Purpose

When you are sitting there pondering your purpose;

When you are wondering why you make the choice to take your first inhale of oxygen the next morning after contemplating a whole night of reasons to fight and go on, let me show you some.

A hug from someone that irreplicable in your heart.

Hearing a song that reaches every part of you.

Accomplishing a video game all the way through that so much time was spent on.

Hikes on a breathtaking day, hidden spots you find with your favorite human, that shut out the whole world.

Conversations that make you laugh as you feel like your entire being is falling apart, because that when you know someone truly cares.

Feel that? It's your heart beating, that has every purpose in the world. And the world is within you. So, take it head on, with every breath, with every beat, your purpose is you.

Ponder that.

Belong

When I feel like the world is against me and I need to leave, I tell myself this is just an emotion at this moment. It comes and goes, it passes, sometimes it lingers longer, and I battle it for days and maybe even months as it whispers to me, and it may come back and say mean things to me like a bully. But that doesn't mean that you need to give that voice power, that voice hold lies. You belong here just as much as everyone else on this planet. And don't you ever forget that.

Tending

Remember that you deserve to be taken care of as well.

Nothing separates you from your needs vs anyone else's needs they both matter just the same.

We often forget about that.

Nurturance is important.

If we do not tend to ourselves, we run on empty and that does not benefit anyone including yourself.

Tending to you makes a difference between just living life, or actually being alive.

Anyone can just drift along through their life, but it takes resilience to be alive and feel alive.

Remind yourself it is your life, body, and mind that should be treasured.

You are just as important as the rest of us.

—Tend to, live, and be alive.

Autumn

I like that she listens to indie music.

I like that she can read all through the night until the AM.

When people doubt her ability to love, she loves harder anyway.

She enjoys the warmth on her face when the sun hits her skin.

She doesn't know what version of herself she will wake up to everyday.

Whether today is the heartache version or the version in which she sees potential,

She is at the mercy of emotions and life's unpredictability.

Her favorite season is autumn.

Forever changing, just like her.

Every day is different and brings new growth to oneself.

We learn new things we didn't know before.

We are taught things by the generations before us. Our planet always changes, and that gives us new opportunities to learn.

Just like yourself, there are always new things to find within.

Different shades of color like fall leaves.

Whatever your story is, just know that the main character matters. In every single way. Other people's choices will affect you but during those times, Remember:

Find Comfort Within the Chaos.

— Em

Notes:

www.ingramcontent.com/pod-product-compliance
Lightning Source LLC
Chambersburg PA
CBHW060528080526
44586CB00012B/658